A SOLDIER'S SKETCHBOOK

THE ILLUSTRATED FIRST WORLD WAR DIARY OF R.H. RABJOHN

JOHN WILSON

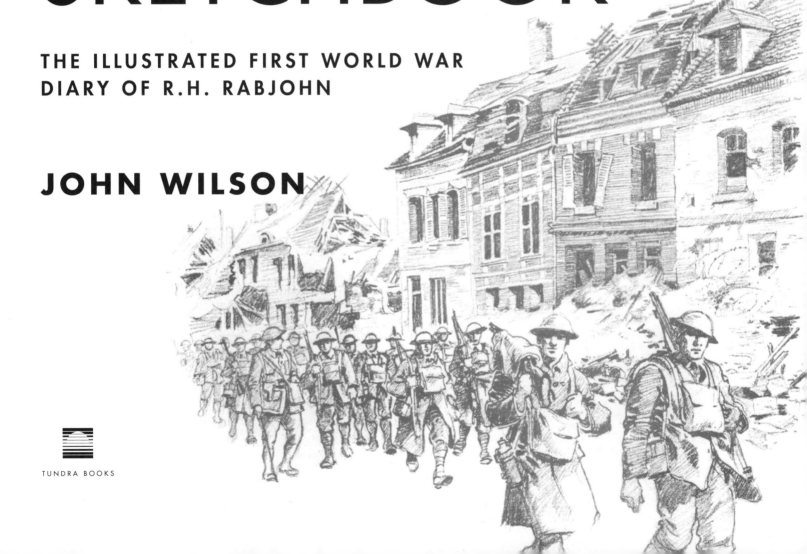

TUNDRA BOOKS

Tundra Books, a division of Random House of Canada Limited, a Penguin Random House Company

Library and Archives Canada Cataloguing in Publication

Rabjohn, R. H. (Russell Hughes), 1898–, author
    A soldier's sketchbook : the illustrated First World War diary of R.H. Rabjohn / John Wilson.

Issued in print and electronic formats.
ISBN 978-1-77049-854-9 (hardback).—ISBN 978-1-77049-856-3 (epub)

1. Rabjohn, R. H. (Russell Hughes), 1898- —Juvenile literature. 2. Rabjohn, R. H. (Russell Hughes),
1898- —Diaries. 3. World War, 1914-1918—Personal narratives, Canadian—Juvenile literature.
4. World War, 1914-1918—Canada—Juvenile literature. 5. Soldiers—Canada—Diaries—Juvenile
literature. I. Wilson, John (John Alexander), 1951-, editor II. Title.

D640.R285   2017j940.3092   C2016-900969-6
                                     C2016-900970-X

Published simultaneously in the United States of America by Tundra Books of Northern
New York, a division of Random House of Canada Limited, a Penguin Random House Company

Library of Congress Control Number: 2016933015

ISBN: 978-1-77049-854-9
ebook ISBN: 978-1-77049-856-3

Edited by Janice Weaver
Designed by Jennifer Griffiths, Art direction by Terri Nimmo
Typeset by Tundra Books, Toronto
Printed and bound in China

Tundra Books,
a division of Random House of Canada Limited,
a Penguin Random House Company
www.penguinrandomhouse.ca

1 2 3 4 5   21 20 19 18 17

Penguin
Random
House
TUNDRA BOOKS

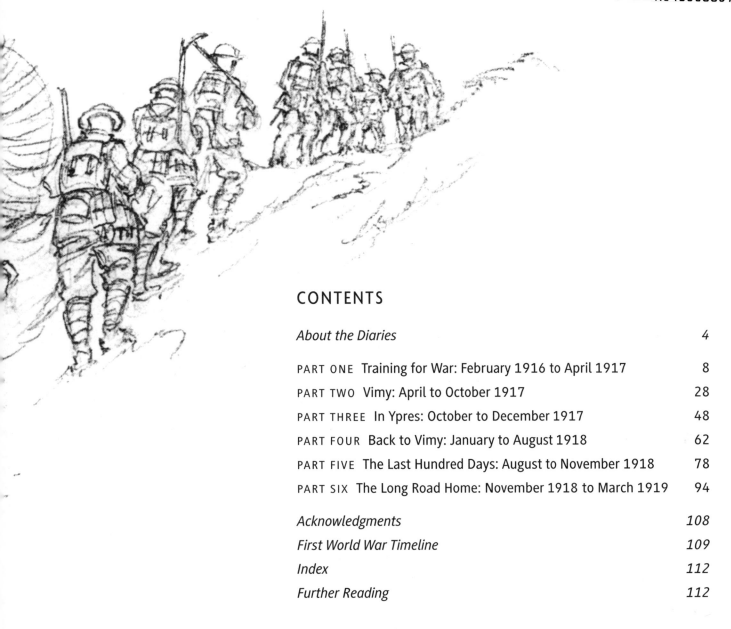

CONTENTS

ABOUT THE DIARIES

The moment I first saw Russell Hughes Rabjohn's remarkable pictures—through a book he published privately in 1977—I knew they were something unique that deserved to be shared. Because First World War soldiers were not permitted to sketch, paint, or take photographs close to the fighting, most images of that conflict were created far from combat. Yet many of Rabjohn's detailed illustrations are scenes of the dangerous front-line world where soldiers lived and died.

Russell Rabjohn was a trained artist when he went to war. Because of this, he was employed to map trenches, draw dugouts, and sketch the graves of his fallen comrades. This allowed him to carry a large artist's sketchbook on the battlefield, and he used this freedom to capture his experiences—the defeated look of a downed German pilot; the ruined buildings and devastated landscapes of the war zone; the endless digging and repairing of

trenches; and the jubilant mood in the streets when the Armistice is finally signed. When he came home, he reworked these sketches and created more, and these form the backbone of the diary you now hold in your hands.

But Rabjohn's incredible illustrations are not his only achievement. In the archives of the Canadian War Museum in Ottawa, I found five written diaries covering his wartime experiences. These diaries are small—designed to be hidden in a uniform pocket—and the events of an entire day must be crammed into a tiny space. Throughout the war, in the damp cellars of bombed-out buildings or in muddy dugouts with bombs and shells exploding nearby, Russell wrote in these diaries. He wrote in pen or pencil and tried to add to his diary every day. But sometimes circumstances prevented this and he had to fill in days whenever an opportunity presented itself. He wrote to remember, so that he could later rework his rough sketches and recreate scenes that he had no chance to draw at the time.

During the days I spent reading Russell's diaries at the Canadian War Museum, I came to know him as an eighteen-year-old boy enthusiastically joining the army in 1916, and as a battle-hardened twenty-one-year-old man coming home again in 1919. The young Russell's diaries are a product of their time. In Ontario in 1914, kids could stop attending school at age fourteen. Russell probably left then to begin training for his art career. Consequently, his grasp of grammar and his spelling skills were shaky. In his original diaries, he often used "I seen" for "I saw," and he made no distinction between "their," "there," and "they're." He rarely used commas and frequently wrote in sentence fragments. When he felt there should be a pause, he inserted a period, but with no capital letter after it. The spelling of some words had him struggling, and the names of French and Belgian villages often left him completely at sea.

Except where I felt that Russell's eccentricities added immediacy to his tale, I have edited out his quirks, correcting his spelling and grammar, putting his words into sentences or more coherent sentence fragments, and more carefully identifying the towns and villages where he found himself. On a few occasions, for the sake of clarity, I have inserted words in square brackets.

At the start of each section, I have provided background information, describing events that were taking place elsewhere as the war dragged on year after year. I also introduce each page of diary entries and insert occasional connecting sentences to help readers understand anything that was left unsaid. But as much as possible, I have simply let the diaries speak for themselves. This is Russell's story and the story of the times he lived in.

PART ONE
TRAINING FOR WAR

FEBRUARY 1916 TO APRIL 1917

HOW RUSSELL'S WAR BEGAN

Shortly before eleven o'clock on the morning of June 28, 1914, on a street in the city of Sarajevo, in Bosnia, a nineteen-year-old Serbian nationalist named Gavrilo Princip fired two pistol shots into an open car stopped on the street in front of him. The shots killed Archduke Franz Ferdinand, the heir to the throne of the Austro-Hungarian Empire, and his wife, Sophie. In revenge, Austria attacked Serbia. To protect Serbia, Russia declared war on Austria. To help Austria, Germany declared war on Russia. To help Russia, France went to war with Germany. To help France, Britain and Canada declared war on Germany.

Within six weeks of Princip's shots, the whole of Europe was at war.

Canada's army in 1914 numbered only 3,110 men and was a long way from the battlefields of Europe. While the vast armies of Germany, France, and Russia fought enormous battles and lost tens of thousands of men, the first Canadian soldiers were still being organized into regiments and transported to Halifax to board ships for England. By April 1915, when the Canadians first saw battle near the Belgian town of Ypres, the war had deteriorated into a long line of opposing trenches stretching from Belgium to Switzerland. Despite battles bigger than anything the world had seen before—and millions of casualties—those trenches barely moved for the next four years.

On February 22, 1916, Russell Rabjohn became a part of this war.

AN ARTIST IS BORN

Russell Rabjohn was born in a modest house on a tree-lined street in Toronto on the first day of January 1898. His childhood was spent in a busy household with two sisters and five brothers. As one of the youngest children, Russell often had to make his own entertainment and soon developed a sharp eye for observing the people around him. In 1908, for his tenth birthday, he was given a copy of *Our Boys and Girls Painting Book*, and he was set on his life's course.

Russell's birthday present had pictures on the left page that the reader was meant to copy as exactly as possible on the right. The subjects ranged from ink drawings of faces, animals, buildings, and cartoon characters to full-colour paintings of scenes.

Copying is a good way to improve skills, but Russell felt it cramped his creativity.

He rarely completed a full page of illustrations, preferring instead to select a single object that caught his attention and copy that. As his skills improved, he began creating his own characters and scenes, including a humorous self-portrait of an ink-stained boy drawing a sketch of his father.

At the age of fourteen, Russell took his love of drawing to the next stage, attending the Ontario College of Art. In 1914, as the world descended into war, he won the Toronto Boys' Dominion Exhibition Award for pen-and-ink drawing.

At sixteen, Russell was too young to become a soldier, but he watched as thousands of other Canadians went overseas to an uncertain future.

ORIGINAL
No. 862539

ATTESTATION PAPER.
180th Battn.

CANADIAN OVER-SEAS EXPEDITIONARY FORCE.

1   Folio.

QUESTIONS TO BE PUT BEFORE ATTESTATION.
(ANSWERS.)

1. What is your surname?		R A B J O H N .
1a. What are your Christian names?		Russell Hughes
1b. What is your present address?		83 Massey St. Toronto Ont.
2. In what Town, Township or Parish, and in what Country were you born?		Toronto, Ont. Can.
3. What is the name of your next-of-kin?		Mary Rabjohn
4. What is the address of your next-of-kin?		83 Massey St. Toronto Ont. Can.
4a. What is the relationship of your next-of-kin?		Mother
5. What is the date of your birth?		Jan. 1, 1898
6. What is your Trade or Calling?		Illustrating
7. Are you married?		No
8. Are you willing to be vaccinated or re-vaccinated and inoculated?		Yes
9. Do you now belong to the Active Militia?		No
10. Have you ever served in any Military Force? (If so, state particulars of former Service.)		No
11. Do you understand the nature and terms of your engagement?		Yes
12. Are you willing to be attested to serve in the CANADIAN OVER-SEAS EXPEDITIONARY FORCE?		Yes

DECLARATION TO BE MADE BY MAN ON ATTESTATION.

I, Russell Hughes Rabjohn, do solemnly declare that the above are answers made by me to the above questions, and that they are true, and that I am willing to fulfil the engagements by me now made, and I hereby engage and agree to serve in the Canadian Over-Seas Expeditionary Force, and to be attached to any arm of the service therein, for the term of one year, or during the war now existing between Great Britain and Germany should that war last longer than one year, and for six months after the termination of that war provided His Majesty should so long require my services, or until legally discharged.

Russell Hughes Rabjohn (Signature of Recruit)

W H Edmiston (Signature of Witness)

Date 22nd February 1916

OATH TO BE TAKEN BY MAN ON ATTESTATION.

I, Russell Hughes Rabjohn, do make Oath, that I will be faithful and bear true Allegiance to His Majesty King George the Fifth, His Heirs and Successors, and that I will as in duty bound honestly and faithfully defend His Majesty, His Heirs and Successors, in Person, Crown and Dignity, against all enemies, and will observe and obey all orders of His Majesty, His Heirs and Successors, and of all the Generals and Officers set over me. So help me God.

R H Rabjohn (Signature of Recruit)

W H Edmiston (Signature of Witness)

Date 22nd February 1916

CERTIFICATE OF MAGISTRATE.

The Recruit above-named was cautioned by me that if he made any false answer to any of the above questions he would be liable to be punished as provided in the Army Act.

The above questions were then read to the Recruit in my presence.

I have taken care that he understands each question, and that his answer to each question has been duly entered as replied to, and the said Recruit has made and signed the declaration and taken the oath before me, at Toronto this 22nd day of February 1916

M-Sweeny (Signature of Justice)

M. F. W. 23.
6003M.—1-15.
H. Q. 1772-30-541.

QUADILPUP

Description of Russell Hughes Rabjohn on Enlistment.

Apparent Age	18 years 1 months. (To be determined according to the instructions given in the Regulations for Army Medical Services.)	Distinctive marks, and marks indicating congenital peculiarities or previous disease.
		(Should the Medical Officer be of opinion that the recruit has served before, he will notice that acknowledge in any previous service, attach a slip to that effect, for the information of the Approving Officer.)
Height	5 ft. 7½ ins.	
Chest measurement { Girth when fully expanded	36 ins.	
Range of expansion	3 ins.	
Complexion	Medium	Mole on left thigh.
Eyes	Blue	Mole on right hip.
Hair	Brown	
Religious denomination:		
Church of England		
Presbyterian		
Methodist	Meth.	
Baptist or Congregationalist		
Roman Catholic		
Jewish		
Other denominations (Denomination to be stated.)		

CERTIFICATE OF MEDICAL EXAMINATION.

I have examined the above-named Recruit and find that he does not present any of the causes of rejection specified in the Regulations for Army Medical Services.

He can see at the required distance with either eye; his heart and lungs are healthy; he has the free use of his joints and limbs, and he declares that he is not subject to fits of any description.

I consider him* fit for the Canadian Over-Seas Expeditionary Force.

Date 22nd February 1916

Place Toronto

[signature] Captain
Medical Officer.

Toronto Recruiting Depot

*Insert here "fi" or "unfit".

NOTE.—Should the Medical Officer consider the Recruit unfit, he will fill in the foregoing Certificate only in the case of those who have attested, and will briefly state below the causes of unfitness.

CERTIFICATE OF OFFICER COMMANDING UNIT.

Russell Hughes Rabjohn having been finally approved and inspected this day, and his Name, Age, Date of Attestation, and every prescribed particular having been complied with, I certify that I am satisfied with the correctness of this Attestation.

A H O'Brien Major (Signature of Officer)
for O.C. Comdg. 180th O.S. Battalion, C.E.F.

Date Feb. 23rd 1916

OFF TO WAR

On the first day of 1916, Rabjohn turned eighteen, making him old enough to join the army. On February 22, he hugged his mother, Mary, and went to the local recruiting office. There he gave his personal details: height, five feet seven inches (1.70 metres); eyes, blue; hair, brown.

He then signed an attestation paper, a form soldiers filled out when they enlisted, declaring that he was agreeing to "serve in the Canadian Over-Seas Expeditionary Force . . . for the term of one year, or during the war now existing between Great Britain and Germany should that war last longer than one year." He identified himself as an illustrator, and revealed that he had moles on his left thigh and right hip—marks that could be used to identify him if he were killed in action.

He promised also to "defend His Majesty . . . against all enemies," a serious responsibility for a kid from Toronto. By day's end, Russell Hughes Rabjohn was Private Rabjohn, service number 862539, in the 180th (Sportsmen) Battalion. On March 29, Russell was joined in the 180th by his thirty-year-old brother, Richard.

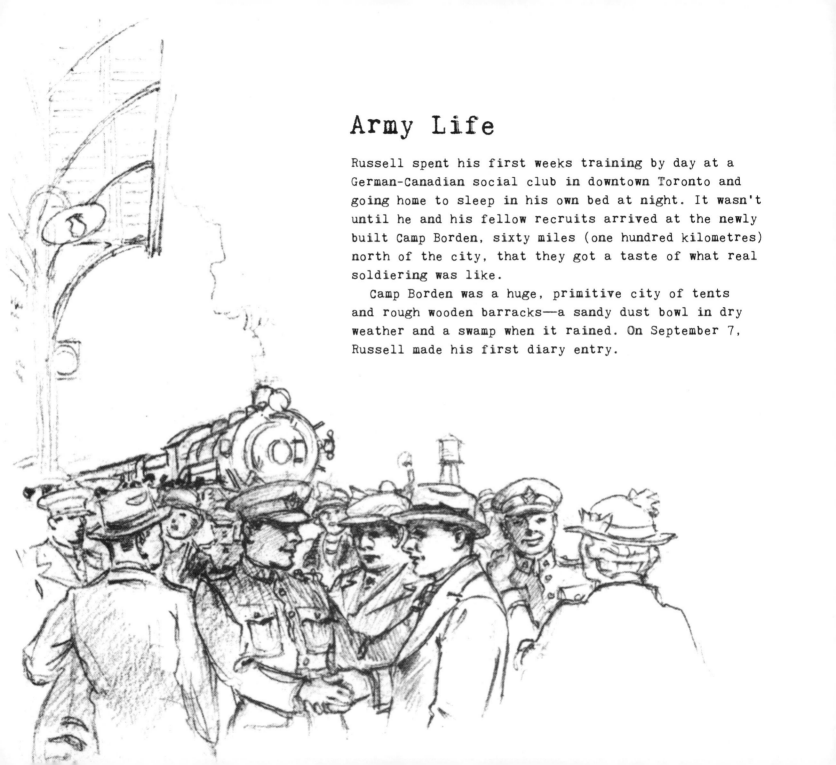

Army Life

Russell spent his first weeks training by day at a German-Canadian social club in downtown Toronto and going home to sleep in his own bed at night. It wasn't until he and his fellow recruits arrived at the newly built Camp Borden, sixty miles (one hundred kilometres) north of the city, that they got a taste of what real soldiering was like.

   Camp Borden was a huge, primitive city of tents and rough wooden barracks—a sandy dust bowl in dry weather and a swamp when it rained. On September 7, Russell made his first diary entry.

THURSDAY, SEPTEMBER 7, 1916

On our way to put the day and night in at the trenches. Had sham fight with 205th [Battalion]. Camp Borden.

Much of the time at Camp Borden was spent on drills, route marches, and musketry and bayonet practice, but there were also concerts, boxing matches, and even trips to Toronto for the occasional weekend leave. In early October, Russell apparently enjoyed his leave a little too much.

MONDAY, OCTOBER 9, 1916

Stayed over my leave till this morning. Absent from 9 p.m. Sunday until 10 a.m. Monday. Fined two days' pay and admonished.

Russell made just one more visit home, in mid-October.

WEDNESDAY, OCTOBER 18, 1916

Started back to camp about 10 p.m. Seen the old folks as I left, and perhaps for last time. Arrived in camp about 1:30 a.m., everything very quiet.

SUNDAY, OCTOBER 22, 1916

Packing up in morning for overseas. Left camp 2:30 p.m., arrived Union Station 5:15. Seen all the folks—they all felt pretty bad at Dick and I leaving.

That day, Russell and his brother said their tearful farewells to family and friends in Toronto and headed east toward the war.

Heading Overseas

As the men travelled, people came out and cheered them on their way. In Saint John, New Brunswick, there were more weeks of drills and marches, but there were also moving picture shows at the Imperial Theatre and Chinese meals for sixty cents. Soon, Russell and his comrades were on their way to Halifax and the ship that would carry them overseas.

MONDAY, NOVEMBER 13, 1916
Arrived in Halifax 5 a.m., was put on boat *Olympic* [the sister ship to the ill-fated *Titanic*] at 1:30 p.m. [Battalions] 194, 222, 147, 194, 173 are also on board, along with a cycle corps, two batteries, and medical staff, with a crew of about eight hundred.

TUESDAY, NOVEMBER 14, 1916
Still on the boat in Halifax. Very heavy snowstorm, about six inches [fifteen centimetres] deep, the first snow of the season. Sailed from Halifax 3:45 p.m. Passed a destroyer about 4:30 p.m. Halifax all blockaded with torpedo nets.

FRIDAY, NOVEMBER 17, 1916
Weather very calm. Had fire drill, saw a few fish jumping out of the water.

SATURDAY, NOVEMBER 18, 1916
Fine in morning, getting stormy toward afternoon and evening. Quite stormy at night and very dark. Phosphorous was very plain, and it was terrible windy.

SUNDAY, NOVEMBER 19, 1916
Windy in morning. Saw first bit of land 8 a.m. Passed through coast of Ireland and Scotland during the morning . . . Passed quite a few destroyers, had two for escort during the afternoon. Anchored during the night in the River Mersey.

MONDAY, NOVEMBER 20, 1916
Arrived in Liverpool docks and anchored 8:30 a.m. Held on boat on account of troop train. Very foggy. Saw Ephal Tower and docks of Liverpool. Very busy place.

"Ephal" is Russell's attempt to spell Eiffel. He is mistaking the New Brighton Tower in Liverpool for the more famous one in Paris. Such was a young Torontonian's view of the world in 1916.

SMALL BOX RESPIRATOR 1916

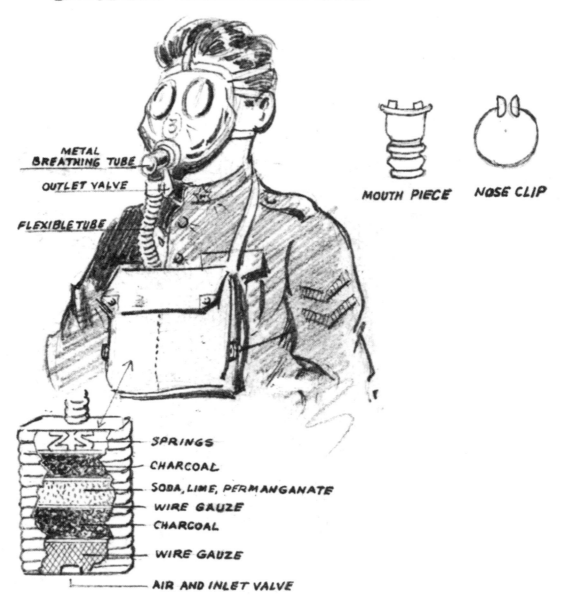

MOUTH PIECE   NOSE CLIP

METAL
BREATHING TUBE

OUTLET VALVE

FLEXIBLE TUBE

SPRINGS

CHARCOAL

SODA, LIME, PERMANGANATE

WIRE GAUZE

CHARCOAL

WIRE GAUZE

AIR AND INLET VALVE

Training Camp

At Shoreham Camp outside Brighton, on England's south
coast, Russell settled into a monotonous routine.
Reveille (the morning bugle call) woke him at 6:30 a.m.,
breakfast was an hour later, and then he had drills
from nine to twelve. After lunch, he had two more hours
of drilling, followed by supper and free time. Lights
out was at 9:45 p.m.

TUESDAY, NOVEMBER 28, 1916
Physical drill, company drill, kit inspection in afternoon . . .
Was down to the town at night with laundry.

WEDNESDAY, NOVEMBER 29, 1916
Weather dry. Physical drill in morning, company drill for later
part of morning. Route march through Kingston by the Sea,
coming through Shoreham back to barracks.

In January, Russell and the others were
reorganized into the 3rd Canadian Reserve
Battalion and moved to West Sandling Camp
outside Folkestone, on the southeastern
coast. It was here that Russell's artistic
talents were first recognized, and he
was asked to paint some large posters to
illustrate training lectures.

THURSDAY, FEBRUARY 1, 1917
Sent for by bombing officers, was asked if I could sketch . . .
Officer showed me what he wanted. We went to the camp

stores [to get] material, went up on hill to bombing school.
I saw exactly what was wanted, got pioneers [soldiers who
perform engineering and building tasks] to make frame for
painting on six by four feet [1.8 metres by 1.2 metres].

FRIDAY, FEBRUARY 2, 1917
Reveille 4:30 a.m. Left camp 6:30 a.m. [and] went over to
the office, then to pioneers. Got frame, took it back to office,
and started on Mills hand grenade, sketching it with oil
paints on canvas, making it about eight times the actual
size of the grenade. Stopped work 4 p.m. Officer seemed
quite satisfied.

In fact, the officer in charge was more
than satisfied—he was so pleased with
the work that he gave Russell several
days of leave to visit London.

On Leave

Leave in London was a big thrill
for a kid from Toronto, and Russell
filled his time to the maximum. He
saw the sights—Buckingham Palace,
London Bridge, the zoo, Madame
Tussauds wax museum—and took in
movies and vaudeville (musical
theatre) shows.

SATURDAY, MARCH 17, 1917
Left camp on six-day pass. Arrived in London about 10 a.m.,
fine scenery along the route . . . Took underground railway
to Piccadilly, am staying at Victoria Club. After dinner took
walk around Piccadilly Circus, Leicester Square, and
Nelson [Trafalgar] Square, then to museum of models of
old guns, ships, torpedoes, etc. Then to the Thames River,
had a look at the Houses of Parliament—a very fine
building—was then shown through the building by a guide.
Saw the coronation chair in which the king and queen sit
at the opening of Parliament, and where King Edward VII
lay in state. Also hung my hat on Lord Kitchener's and
Lord Roberts's pegs.

SUNDAY, MARCH 18, 1917
Got up about 9 a.m., went out, had shoeshine. Took a
walk around Oxford Circus, took bus to London Bridge
[and then to] Westminster Abbey, Houses of Parliament,
etc. From there around through Victoria Station, took
walk through Petticoat Lane [a famous
street market]. Everything hauled out on
street same as weekday. Took bus up to
Bank of England—a very fine building with
large dome. Pigeons by the hundreds will
feed out of your hand. From there . . . went to
Westminster Abbey . . . the finest building I
ever saw in my life.

TUESDAY, MARCH 20, 1917
Got up 9:30, took walk through Oxford Circus way. Saw
about two hundred people lined up for potatoes. Went to
zoo, made sketch of figure "stealing the cubs." Very heavy
rainstorm in afternoon. Went to show in afternoon and
evening. Very few Canadians in London at present—all
New Zealanders, Australian, French, and Belgians.

But after weeks of sketching posters
and six days of leave, Russell had a
hard time getting back to training as
a soldier.

FRIDAY, MARCH 23, 1917
Reveille 5:30 a.m. Moved off to ranges 7 a.m. Fine
morning so far. The pack seemed very heavy after not
having one on for over six weeks.

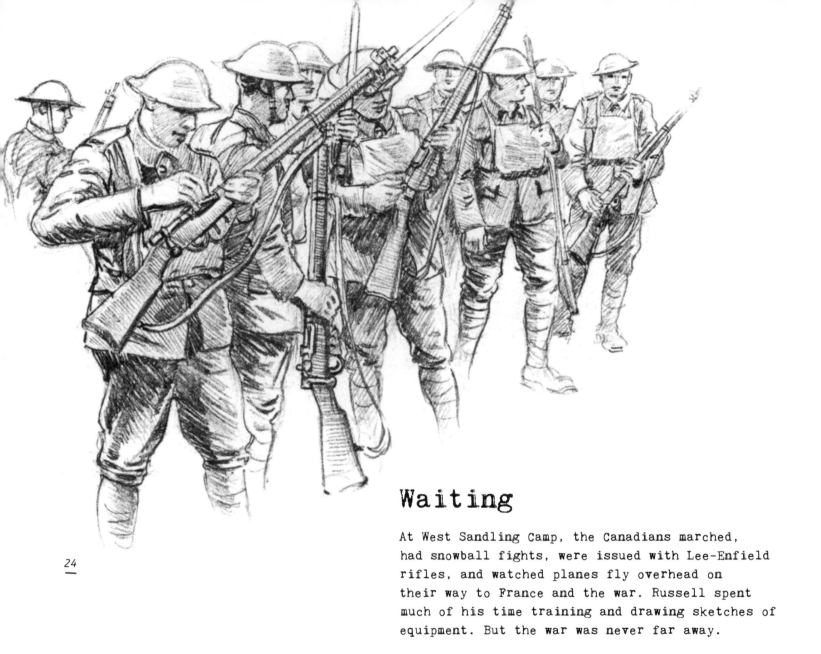

Waiting

At West Sandling Camp, the Canadians marched,
had snowball fights, were issued with Lee-Enfield
rifles, and watched planes fly overhead on
their way to France and the war. Russell spent
much of his time training and drawing sketches of
equipment. But the war was never far away.

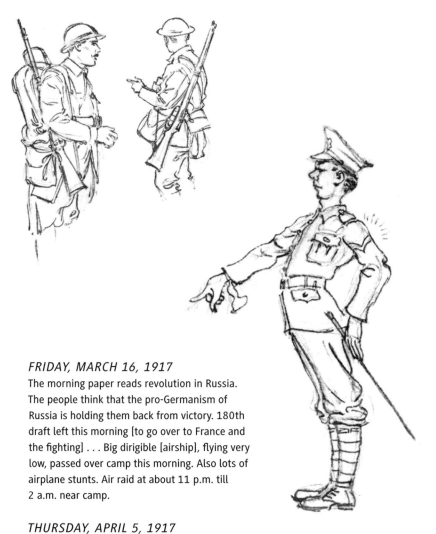

FRIDAY, APRIL 6, 1917

Brigadier died today from accident yesterday. Church parade in morning, dismissed for rest of day . . . Confined to barracks, awaiting draft. Stayed in hut nearly all day. At night most of the fellows felt pretty good, so we had lots of music and stories, especially from Statts the Indian, an old circus hand. And Brise, who is not all there, gave us a few acrobatic stunts.

SATURDAY, APRIL 7, 1917

Physical drill in morning, kit inspection by Captain Duncan. Was then put on fatigue sweeping out one of the huts. The lieutenant in charge passed cigarettes around. We were then paraded for bombing. Went to the range bombing area, after which we had bayonet fighting. America declares war on Germany today, seizes eighty ships.

FRIDAY, MARCH 16, 1917

The morning paper reads revolution in Russia. The people think that the pro-Germanism of Russia is holding them back from victory. 180th draft left this morning [to go over to France and the fighting] . . . Big dirigible [airship], flying very low, passed over camp this morning. Also lots of airplane stunts. Air raid at about 11 p.m. till 2 a.m. near camp.

THURSDAY, APRIL 5, 1917

Had kit inspection, supplied with two hundred rounds ammunition. Had brigade mobilization in afternoon, ready to move any place. After being dismissed about 3:10 p.m., we fell in 4:10 p.m. for musketry . . . The brigadier fell off his horse, fractured his skull.

At Last

As spring arrived, Russell was "warned for the
draft," or told that he would soon be shipped
over to France. Arrangements were made—Russell
had his hair clipped and was issued with an
identification disc—but there were still delays.
It was immensely frustrating, and the men engaged
in a lot of drinking and fighting. It was a
miserable few weeks.

SUNDAY, APRIL 8, 1917

Easter Sunday, the time is put back one hour to allow more daylight for the summer months. Paraded to church. We are still held in barracks, expect to go to France in morning. Very fine spring day.

TUESDAY, APRIL 10, 1917

Physical drill, OC [officer commanding] inspection, then paraded up to area. Had squad drill, bayonet fighting, over the hurdles. Came back about 11:30 a.m., had inspection. Twenty-eight men put in waiting on the draft, the remainder of the camp was rehearsing. Funeral parade for late Brigadier Buel.

THURSDAY, APRIL 12, 1917

Physical drill, OC inspection, bombing, squad drill, bayonet fighting. Very fine day. In afternoon had bayonet fighting over the jumps, lecture by Lieutenant Morrow as to difficulties at the front, then some more squad drill.

FRIDAY, APRIL 13, 1917

Physical drill, OC parade. Still waiting draft. Bayonet fighting, bombing, squad drill, route march in afternoon through Saltwood, Hythe, Lympne, Lyminge. Was very tired and feet very sore. Stayed in at night.

SATURDAY, APRIL 14, 1917

Physical drill, OC parade, then bayonet fighting, bombing. Held in all afternoon. Had inspection. Played cards all evening—mostly poker. Four MPs raided the hut. It ended up all right, but was warned.

SUNDAY, APRIL 15, 1917

Church parade in morning. Was talking to some of the 198 Buffs [the 198th Overseas Battalion, known as the Canadian Buffs], who were over to our camp for a bath. Had inspection and muster roll call in afternoon. Stayed in hut the rest of time, still waiting draft. Thurtleson, one of our boys in the hut, was arrested as a spy. He was the means of the arrest of Muller in London, who was shot.

On April 18, Russell was finally marched to Folkestone and boarded a ship to cross the English Channel. He was to join the 123rd Pioneer Battalion, Royal Grenadiers, in the 3rd Infantry Division of the Canadian Expeditionary Force. The diary entry for that day was headed, in bold capitals, "ARRIVED IN FRANCE." At last, Russell was going to war.

PART TWO

VIMY

APRIL TO OCTOBER 1917

THE WAR AROUND RUSSELL

Russell arrived at the war in late April 1917 during the Battle of Arras, a massive Allied offensive near the northern French city of that name. In the first phase of the battle, the Canadian Corps was given the job of assaulting a vital ridge near the village of Vimy. That attack—on April 9, Easter Monday—was a dramatic success and cemented the Canadians' reputation as shock troops. The victory also gave all Canadians a sense of pride, and the huge memorial that today stands on Vimy Ridge symbolizes the beginnings of Canadian nationhood.

Unfortunately, when Russell arrived at Vimy, the larger Battle of Arras had descended into another slogging match where little was gained in exchange for a huge daily increase in the lists of dead and wounded. After almost 160,000 Allied casualties, the battle petered out in mid-May.

As Russell learned about war in the area around Vimy in the summer of 1917, he heard about another battle, near the town of Ypres, fifty miles (eighty kilometres) to the north. The battle began on July 31 and Russell followed news of it with interest. He didn't know that it was called the Third Battle of Ypres, or that it would become much better known as Passchendaele.

He also didn't suspect that the Battle of Passchendaele would last for more than three months, and that eventually he and the other members of the 123rd Battalion would be drawn into its horrors.

Arrived in France

The moment Russell set foot in France—on April 18, 1917—his handwriting became smaller and more intense. It's almost as if he was struggling to pack all his new experiences onto the cramped pages of his diary. Although he was still a long way from the front lines, the war suddenly seemed more real.

THURSDAY, APRIL 19, 1917
No bugle calls in this camp. Breakfast 7 a.m., inspected, medical. I ducked the parade on account of having scabies [an itchy skin rash]. During the night you could hear the big guns very distinct. Heavy bombardment going on.

Over the next two days, Russell marched through Boulogne and boarded a train south to Le Havre. It was a journey of only 155 miles (250 kilometres), but it took twenty-two uncomfortable hours.

SATURDAY, APRIL 21, 1917
Left Boulogne about 5:30 p.m. [in a] very large troop train, mostly plain boxcars, forty-eight [soldiers] in one car. Nothing to eat for supper . . . Quite a few tunnels during the trip . . . one in which we were stalled and nearly smothered with gas. Passed quite a few very large camps and hospitals . . . Very little sleep at night, had no place to lie. Too crowded.

SUNDAY, APRIL 22, 1917

Still in the old boxcar, [along with] three cars of German prisoners, very dirty-looking. Breakfast consisted of hard tack, bully beef, and a little jam . . . Every kid as the train would slacken down wanted bully beef or a biscuit. Arrived in Le Havre about 3:15 p.m. Very nice-looking camp but terrible crowded.

At Le Havre, Russell was issued a gas mask, a rifle and bayonet, 120 rounds of ammunition, and a three-day ration of sugar, tea, bully beef, biscuits, jam, and cheese. On April 24, he and his fellow soldiers headed inland, at first by train and then on foot.

WEDNESDAY, APRIL 25, 1917

Very heavy march led by a boy guide . . . Was billeted at Gauchin-Légal in old barns, nice running creek alongside us for washing. You could hear guns and see the reflections very plain during the night. Put in very good night's sleep. Ready for fifteen-mile [twenty-four-kilometre] march tomorrow.

THURSDAY, APRIL 26, 1917

Got up about 9:30 a.m., had a little bully beef, washed in running creek alongside farmhouse, started march for Arras at 9:45. Very long hill to start, with a heavy load. Passed a few German prisoners . . . three dead horses, a few broken guns. Passed through Mont-Saint-Éloi, [with its] old church all battered from shells . . . Reached the camp of 123rd [Battalion] about 5:30 p.m. . . . Watched airplanes up over the trenches being fired at; two were brought down that I saw in a cloud of smoke. We're camping in tents and dugouts. Guns are just a little ways off from us, can see them firing very plainly. Heavy shelling during the night.

33

Living Conditions

Once Russell and his mates got to the front, their job was to consolidate the ground that the Canadians had won in the previous weeks. This involved digging and repairing trenches and dugouts, as well as creating a light railway to carry supplies to the front lines. For their first few weeks, the Battle of Arras still raged around them, making their work extremely dangerous and giving Russell his first taste of death.

SATURDAY, APRIL 28, 1917

Got up 3 a.m., had breakfast. Moved off 4 a.m. up the line for work. Very dark. About 4:30 a.m., the Canadians opened up a barrage on Frizs [Russell's version of "Fritz," slang for the Germans]. The noise was awful. We were walking up the railroad tracks over no man's land . . . which the Germans held two weeks ago . . . No man's land is a mess of ruins, holes and dugouts, old rifles, guns, bombs, scattered all over . . . Frizs put a few big ones [artillery shells] over our head . . . Just a horse killed.

MONDAY, APRIL 30, 1917

Got up 8 a.m., paraded down to gas school for box respirator . . . The road down to the school is nothing but a mass of ruins made into dugouts . . . Transports by the hundreds coming and going every now and again. A graveyard of our boys with wooden crosses erected . . . The bunch was shelled pretty hard today—a couple got blightys [slang for a wound that will take the soldier home] in the behind. Frizs was also sailing over our camp tonight; our machines got after him, he soon got over on his own side.

TUESDAY, MAY 1, 1917

Early this morning, Frizs let one of his big shells light in Mont-Saint-Éloi, burying about twenty headquarters band. In the afternoon, about 4 p.m., an old French bomb pit about fifty yards [forty-five metres] from our tent blew up, making a hole seven times the size of a bell tent. Injured about three. One sergeant got a bad crack in the head, another got shell-shocked. As far as they know, two fellows had a fire right on that bit of ground where it blew up, so they think the two fellows went up with it. As soon as the explosion occurred, everybody made for the trenches with their gas masks on.

WEDNESDAY, MAY 2, 1917

Heavy barrages again this morning. There's no limit to our shells, and Frizs knows it. Went up the line just this side of Vimy Ridge at 11 a.m., worked unloading cars till 7:30 p.m. . . . About 9 p.m. we were in bed when one of the Frizs airplanes gave us a little surprise—passed right over our camp very low, dropped about a dozen bombs, killed two transport fellows, injuring about eight. Our machine guns played heavy on him, but he got away. Everybody made for the trenches when they heard him.

Death
All Around

In the midst of all the chaos, Russell and his comrades had to find a ruined rat-infested cellar, an abandoned German dugout, or a crumbling cave and create a secure home. Sometimes, they were not too secure.

MONDAY/TUESDAY, MAY 7/8, 1917

Frizs . . . let us have it at the cave good and proper. Sent over gas with it. He busted one cave in, hurting three of our platoon—partly burying them, busting their legs, and giving two of them shrapnel. One of our boys did good work fetching stretchers, etc., under heavy fire. We dug the boys out . . . Our stretcher-bearer made a trip to the dressing station in his bare feet. The mud was up to our neck. Wounded by the dozen [were] coming along the road just by our cave. Frizs gave us lots of gas, killing a few horses, also a couple of drivers.

The war diary for the 123rd Battalion called the shelling "very heavy" and commended the stretcher-bearer for walking "over barb wire, with but his socks on." The war diary also stated that "the others [likely including Russell] acted with equal devotion to duty." Even days later, nothing had calmed down.

FRIDAY, MAY 11, 1917

Frizs gave it to us that heavy we were lucky in getting away safe. The shells were fierce, shrapnel buzzing past us like hummingbirds. He set the bush on fire, in which we were working. We managed to get to the cave okay. Not so bad in the afternoon, so we went ahead with the work in the bush. We're sending over a terrible barrage tonight. Two of our planes also brought down today.

SATURDAY, MAY 12, 1917

Two of the boys were blown to pieces last night. Frizs also sent over a lot of gas, gassed eight of the boys. A couple more were also wounded. His shelling was awful right around our cave. As the gas came, the boys were running in the dark with coats over their heads. The next thing to being all mad.

In ten days, Russell's "A" Company of some 160 men had suffered thirty casualties (dead and wounded).

The Work Must Go On

Through everything, the battalion had to keep working. Most of what Russell and "A" Company did was build and repair the light railways. The work was endless, and even the less dangerous tasks, such as digging to find uncontaminated water, could be extremely unpleasant.

WEDNESDAY, MAY 16, 1917
Working on drains through Thélus [from] 3 a.m. to 12.30 p.m. Very raw cold. A heavy barrage on the right in morning . . . While digging the drains, one of the boys struck a dead horse.

THURSDAY, MAY 17, 1917
Working through Thélus, digging holes for water. No shelling from the German lines. Our guns were pretty lively. One hole we were making must have had dead bodies under it. Stunk terrible.

SUNDAY, MAY 20, 1917
Working on Thélus siding, about 9 a.m. Frizs sent a coal box [a large explosive shell] just over our heads, very near hitting an engine, which soon made out of the way. We stopped work for the time but were sent back again. Then another one hit just short of us, wounding one of our boys in the leg and a couple of Imperials [British troops]. We stopped work and made for the trenches. From then on he put them over by the dozens, breaking up all the light railway tracks and about a dozen cars on the large railway. He put one away over by the nine elms right opposite the siding, blowing up some horses and men.

Fun and Games

When they were not fighting, soldiers
needed to be kept busy, and the men of
the 123rd were particularly good at
baseball and excelled on sports days.
But there were hazards to open-air
sports in daylight.

FRIDAY, MAY 25, 1917
Holiday for our company. Sports in the morning and
band concert, football game in afternoon. Frizs planes
tried to come over all morning but were held back by
our air guns. He was dropping a lot of high explosive
and shrapnel just shy of our camp this afternoon.

SUNDAY, JULY 8, 1917
Extraordinary quiet day, not one gun to be heard.
Raining all last night, very cold through the day. Our big
baseball game came off after tea . . . 40 Battery won
4–2. An awful pile of money lost on the game. During
the fourth inning, a Frizs plane came over—first plane
up during day . . . As soon as he spied the crowd, he
swooped right down at us, firing his machine gun as he
crossed the field. He was no more than twenty yards
[eighteen metres] off the ground. He hit nobody at all.

Many evenings there were band
concerts and stage shows, put on by
the soldiers themselves or travelling
entertainment groups. Behind the lines,
there were *estaminets* (cafes)—many
run out of people's front rooms—where
the soldiers could buy cheap wine,
wolf down some food, and relax.
   Whenever possible, Russell was
up for a game of poker, and his
diary is peppered with comments on
his fortunes: "won twelve francs,"
"lost four francs (as usual)." He also
played craps, horseshoes, and a dice
game called Crown and Anchor. In
nostalgic moments, he listened to a
Victrola, an old-fashioned music
player, which, he said, "brings you
as near home as anything."

A New Job

In mid-June, Russell became a draughtsman.
He was tasked with sketching the trenches,
marking machine gun nests, and mapping the
battalion camps and sports fields. Most of
this work was carried out at headquarters,
but he often had to go forward to observe
what he'd been told to draw. His new job
was less strenuous than building railways,
but not much safer.

MONDAY, JULY 2, 1917
Working on sketch of officers' dugout for Captain Hamilton.
About 10:30 a.m. two German airplanes dived out of the
clouds on one of our scout planes. A battle took place for
fifteen minutes. Our scout managed to get away, but he must
have had a few bullet holes in his plane. Then about 12 p.m.,
seven more of his planes came over very low. Anti-aircraft
guns firing from all directions, also machine guns and rifles.
It was an exciting few minutes. One of our company got hit
with a piece of shrapnel. Only bruised him.

MONDAY, JULY 9, 1917
About 12 a.m., Frizs started shelling . . . Everybody was
making away from the camp [and taking cover] in deep
dugouts, etc. Frenchy and I were jumping the trench as best
we could in the dark—my boots unlaced, sticking in the mud,
shirt all open, and overcoat bundled up in my arm. Frenchy got
hit as we were running. I didn't see . . . He was looked after all
right. Shrapnel was passing me in all directions.

But despite the shelling and the ever-
present danger, there was still time to
take in some entertainment and visit
nearby villages.

SUNDAY, JULY 15, 1917
In afternoon my chum Gerald Burke and I went to Mont-Saint-
Éloi. Was up in the old tower, which has been battered up
during this war. The tower stands on the hill and you can see
all over the country . . . From there, we went to Acq [a nearby
town] . . . bought four rings, had egg supper. An old man came
out beating a drum. These men are used to making as much
noise as possible, get the people out, then give the news.

On top of everything else, that summer
the Germans began using a terrifying new
weapon: mustard gas.

MONDAY, AUGUST 20, 1917
This new gas Frizs is using irritates your skin, as well as [being]
deadly if inhaled, therefore short pants [are] prohibited to
wear when up the line.

43

Prisoners

Like many soldiers, Russell was fascinated
by the enemy. In a war fought mostly from
trenches and dugouts, where the men you were
battling were rarely seen, prisoners took on
a special interest. He first saw some in
Boulogne shortly after he landed in France.

FRIDAY, APRIL 20, 1917

Boulogne, France, is a very lively place but very dirty in places. Seen batch of prisoners marching through town, some very big, ugly-looking brutes among them.

Every time Russell mentioned an Allied attack in his diaries, he carefully noted the number of prisoners taken.

WEDNESDAY, AUGUST 1, 1917

War news good today—the French and Canadians went over on Ypres front, gaining their objective fifteen miles [twenty-four kilometres] wide, three [almost five kilometres] deep, taking at least three thousand prisoners. Tanks did excellent work.

Russell was enthusiastically recording the opening moves of the Battle of Passchendaele. His figures were optimistic, however, and the next day the German counterattack won back most of the lost ground. Later in the year, Russell visited some prisoners in a fenced enclosure where they were kept after capture.

SATURDAY, OCTOBER 27, 1917

The bunch went over again this morning, brought back about 140 prisoners. I was over to the cage to see them—half of them officers and NCOs [non-commissioned officers], four very young boys. Taking them general, they were a pretty fine-looking bunch. About the middle of the morning, twenty [German] planes came over, just dropped a few bombs. The prisoners stood watching them. I made for the open field away from the road.

Even years later, when Russell was reworking a sketch he'd made of some prisoners, he reminisced beside it, "It was always interesting to talk to prisoners. Some worried as to their future, others would like to know if their folks would be notified. All welcomed a cigarette, a fresh drink, or a kind word."

The prisoners were not the only ones seeking information. Sometimes the enemy wanted to know what had happened to their missing men.

MONDAY, OCTOBER 1, 1917

During the afternoon, a red balloon came down, sent from Frizs lines with a note attached asking the whereabouts of a German aviator recently brought down in our lines . . . Today [an enemy] observation balloon got loose. The observer jumped and landed in our lines and is still at large.

Moving Off

Even while the main battle on the
Western Front was raging around Ypres,
Russell's area was far from quiet.

TUESDAY, AUGUST 21, 1917

As soon as we got on top of the ridge, you could see the whole front. Frizs playing hell with a town just to the right of Loos—nothing but a mass of shells bursting. The roads are sheltered by large screens, to avoid observation. After dinner we took the long walk down the ridge, going through several towns before hitting our destination . . . a large mining town no more than four miles [about six kilometres] from the line. Just a very few houses on the outskirts of it [had been] hit. It's been a German residential and mining town—supposed to be practically owned by a German duke. For some reason or other, we didn't shell it. Lots of civilians in it.

But Passchendaele was still grinding on two months later. The growing casualty lists meant replacements were in high demand and the tentacles of war reached out to grab Russell and his battalion. It was their turn to experience the mud and horror of Ypres.

FRIDAY, OCTOBER 19, 1917

Was wakened up 4 a.m. to pack up on the double, which we had to do, having everything ready by 7 a.m. to move off. We [each] had a heavy pack, also our overcoats . . . Traffic was terrible, Imperials and Canadians moving in and New Zealanders and Australians moving out . . . [We got] to our destination by dinner time [in Russell's day, "dinner" was lunch and "supper" was the evening meal], and we had to dig in for ourselves. The place is terrible muddy and it rained hard during the afternoon. Frizs bombed at night. Lights all out.

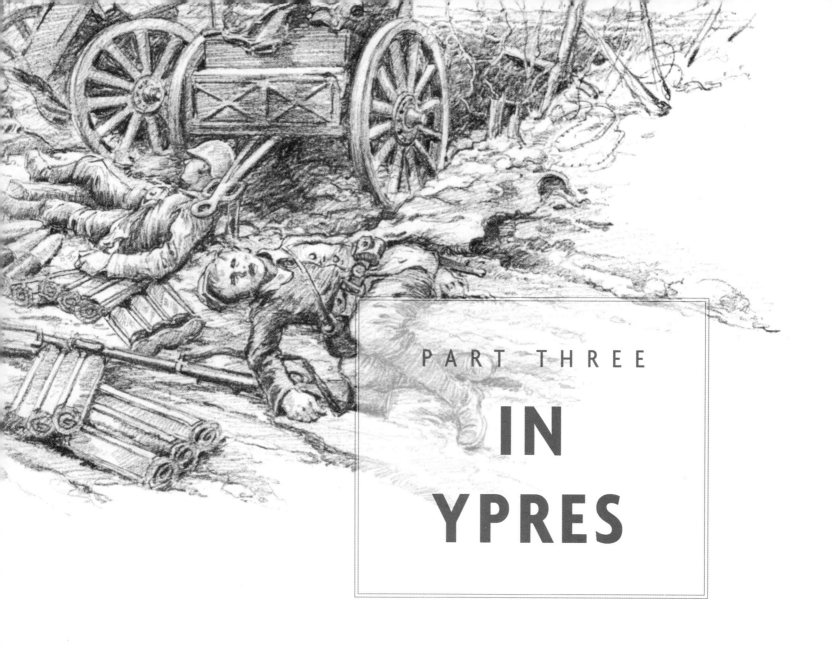

PART THREE

IN YPRES

OCTOBER TO DECEMBER 1917

A STEP-BY-STEP ATTACK

Passchendaele was the third major battle around the town of Ypres, in the Flanders region of Belgium. The first one began on October 19, 1914, when the war was only ten weeks old. It was three years to the day before Russell boarded his train near Arras. The First Battle of Ypres lasted for a month and resulted in fifty-eight thousand dead, wounded, or missing soldiers for the British Expeditionary Force—more than one-third of its strength at the beginning of the battle. On April 22, 1915, the Second Battle of Ypres began. During that month-long engagement, the Germans launched a devastating weapon, poison gas, and it was the first Canadians in France who helped hold the line against this new horror.

In 1917, the ruined town of Ypres was where the British commander, Field Marshal Douglas Haig, decided to push back the enemy. For this Third Battle of Ypres, more commonly known as Passchendaele, the intention was not to break through in a single day, which is what had been tried in previous years, but to fight small battle after small battle with only limited objectives, to eat away at the German lines until they were exhausted. Unfortunately, this type of warfare weakened the attackers as much as it did the defenders.

Nineteen seventeen was a very wet year, and the millions of shells exchanged on the hills above Ypres turned the battlefield into a swamp of mud that stuck to men's boots and sucked careless soldiers and transport horses down to a frightful death. Trenches disappeared, and exhausted, filthy men clung to lines of muddy shell holes and tried to survive. The battle resulted in more than two hundred thousand casualties on each side. This was the horror that Russell entered in October.

51

Flanders Mud

Like countless thousands of others,
Russell had to struggle with the
famously gluey mud of Flanders. It
amazed him so much that he devoted
several pages to it in his diary.

SATURDAY, OCTOBER 20, 1917
We're now at St. Jean, just past Ypres . . . Tanks, airplanes,
war implements of all descriptions lying all over the place.
Tanks being used as dugouts. Charlie Christie got a piece [of
shrapnel] through the left hand. The mud was terrible—mules
stuck, men almost stuck . . . Impossible to dig more than
two feet [sixty centimetres] in the ground for water, as we're
just about the sea level. Any trenches there happen to be are
filled with water. The front line consist[s] of shell holes. The
New Zealanders came here with a division [ten to twelve thousand men] and are going out with not much more than a
brigade [two to four thousand men]. Big howitzers just down
the hill from us mounted on trains, and there are thousands
of guns.

MONDAY, OCTOBER 22, 1917
Lots of mud. My job today consists of making a couple of
sketches of Major Boone, who fell in a shell hole full of mud
and was the next thing to being a goner . . . By the weight of my
boots I'm carrying half of Belgium around with me. I'm mud
from my feet to my head. A poor old mule tied tight to a post
just cross the line gone crazy. No wonder. If I put six months
more in this country, I'll be crazy. I guess the mule is one of the
first contingent.

Horror

In the longest entry in his diary, covering the space normally reserved for two full days, Russell wrote of the effects of the German shelling. Like other soldiers of that time, he didn't talk about his emotions or describe how he felt, but the impact on him is clear in the length of the entry and in his struggle to express the horror he'd witnessed. His descriptions of the consequences of war are sometimes difficult to read.

SUNDAY, OCTOBER 21, 1917

Five of us put the night in a bivouac. Frizs dropped a bunch of bombs, killing one of the "B" Company men in his dugout [but] not scratching his chum, who was sleeping with him . . . After dinner I was sent with two officers to find HQ [headquarters]. As luck would have it, we went off the trail a little ways, ducking as a shell went over. This shell hit on the road a hundred yards [ninety metres] from HQ, lighting up a platoon [forty to fifty men] of "C" Company, killing twenty-seven. The officers wouldn't go up for a time in case [the Germans] shelled again, so an Australian and myself went along the street and looked at the bodies but could identify nobody. Sixteen lay dead, the rest being taken away wounded. Ten dying later on in the hospital . . . One fellow lay cut in half, another head right off, face off, back of head, legs off, arms off. Pieces of bodies lying here and there. Also two touring cars blown up, one still burning while I was there. Our [general service] wagon got a bump, knocking all the officers' kits around. At night I had to make the trip again, taking all the runners to show them where HQ was. [The Germans were] dropping bombs by the dozen in the very place where the men got killed. [One] turned a truck upside down, blowing it to pieces. A very large theatre and cathedral are the main spots of Ypres, all blown to pieces.

Mules and Horses

The First World War was not a mechanized
conflict. The carrying, dragging, pulling,
and lifting were mostly done by the muscles
of men, horses, and mules, and the horror was
there for all of them. In 1917, Britain was
using 530,000 horses and 230,000 mules on the
Western Front alone. Half a million British
horses died in the fighting. Russell's
diaries—like the diaries and letters home
of many soldiers—often mentioned the war-
torn landscape littered with dead animals.

WEDNESDAY, OCTOBER 24, 1917
The sun was shining first thing this morning, so I took a walk over to the YMCA to get some biscuits. The poor old pack mules and horses are lined up both sides of the road while their drivers go and have a cup of tea. They're a solid statue of mud and look worn out. Every now and again, a mule comes along with a piece shot out of him by shrapnel and all covered with blood. The mud is terrible. You never know when you'll drop four or six feet [about one to two metres] by stepping on a piece of soft ground.

Most horses and mules
were killed by shelling or
bombing, but in the special
horror of Passchendaele,
a mule stumbling off one
of the narrow plank roads
stood a good chance of
drowning in the thick mud
that filled every hollow
in the shell-scarred
landscape.

SATURDAY, OCTOBER 27, 1917
Quite cool this morning. The bunch left for their work [at] 3 a.m., up fixing roads, filling shell holes, etc. Mud is terrible. Six or seven stranded tanks put out of action by the mud and shellfire now being used as dugouts. Mules by the hundreds lay dead along the roadsides.

Life and Death

Sometimes, circumstances required
that soldiers take on different roles.
Occasional ceasefires to collect wounded
and bury the dead were not uncommon, and
soldiers like Russell were often
assigned to act as stretcher-bearers.
After a big attack, no man's land could
be thick with the dead and the dying.

WEDNESDAY, OCTOBER 31, 1917
Party left 3 a.m. acting as stretcher-bearers. Frizs and us had armistice [a ceasefire] while [we] were picking up wounded. It was a terrible sight. Frizs party you could see very plain waving a Red Cross flag, six to a stretcher. Made two trips up and back. Some were there until late at night. Nobody hit. Frizs bombed right after dinner, letting one drop [close to] our dugout and making a hole about seven feet [two metres] deep and fifteen feet [more than four metres] in diameter. Nobody hurt. He came over again at night and bombed Ypres. Fifty dead, twenty wounded, and a bunch of horses.

Every day, Russell and his mates
were bombed or shelled. Huge German
bombers called Gothas flew over,
seemingly whenever they wished.
Shells exploded all around. Survival
or death was largely a matter of
luck, and sometimes Russell's diary
reads like a catalogue of his
friends dying.

SATURDAY, NOVEMBER 3, 1917
George Tennant and Olsen killed—Tennant dying immediately, Olsen dying by the time they got him to the dressing station. Tennant got hit in head and chest.

SUNDAY, NOVEMBER 4, 1917
Frizs start[ed] to shell again, keeping it up all night and us in a small dugout [with a] tin roof. One shrapnel ball came through, just missing my head by half a foot [fifteen centimetres], knocking dirt all over my face, and the ball fell on my pillow . . . Simmons and Watson were killed in their dugout, both being cut off at the hips. Killed instantly.

The City of Light

After a month of horror, Russell was
moved away from Ypres in the third week
of November and told he would be sent
back to Vimy. But first, he was granted
a two-week leave. He filled up on a good
breakfast, got a haircut and a shave,
and then embarked for Paris. With its
beautiful parks, quaint streets, and
world-famous sights, the city, he said,
was "a spectacle never to be forgotten."

THURSDAY, NOVEMBER 29, 1917

Went to Versailles, a twelve-mile [nineteen-kilometre] ride on the train, and went all through the palace of Napoleon [Bonaparte] and Marie Antoinette. It occupies acres and acres of grounds. The building is magnificent. Saw all the famous war paintings from the first French war up to Napoleon Bonaparte.

The history and culture of Paris were stunning for a boy from Toronto, which was then a small and unsophisticated city. Between visits to famous sights like the Eiffel Tower and Notre-Dame Cathedral, Russell spent much of each day walking around and soaking up the atmosphere. He visited art galleries and museums, and bought sketchbooks for himself. In the evenings, he dined out and went to the cinema.

MONDAY, DECEMBER 3, 1917

Walked around Paris, then to the Ferris wheel [next to the Eiffel Tower]. Went up on it. Can see all over for miles. Each car will hold thirty people . . . Had dinner at Madame Luisse's [the guest house where he was staying], went to Olympia theatre at night. It was fun.

WEDNESDAY, DECEMBER 5, 1917

Feeling tired as usual, got up at noon. After dinner took walk . . . to Notre-Dame Cathedral . . . Also saw the monument and entrance under the ground in which prisoners were put in olden days and let die.

Despite all he'd seen and experienced, the war was still an interest and he went to see "the Zeppelin brought down near Paris, airplanes, etc. Painting of the trenches, also others—all very good." Eventually, on December 11, he had a farewell drink with the friends he'd made in the city and travelled all night to Amiens to rejoin the fighting.

61

PART FOUR

BACK TO VIMY

JANUARY TO AUGUST 1918

YPRES AND THE PIONEERS

REVALLE 3.A.M.

BREAFAST 4.A.M.

LAYING BATH MATS BY 4.30.A.M. THROUGH THE STREETS OF ST. JEAN.

THEN SAND BAGS FOR SHELL HOLES

BUT THE WORST JOB OF ALL IS PULLING MOKES OUT OF THE MUD.

R.H. RABJOHN YPRES. NOV. 1917

LAST GASPS

In April 1917, the United States had declared war on Germany. With her fresh supplies of soldiers and massive industrial output, this signalled the end for the Germans. The problem for the Allies, though, was that it would take more than a year for the US war machine to get rolling, and for all those men and weapons to make a difference. In the meantime, the Russian Revolution took that important ally out of the war in November 1917, releasing entire German armies from the Eastern Front to fight in France and Belgium.

The Germans had one last chance: if they could destroy the British army before the Americans arrived in numbers, then they might yet win the war.

On March 21, 1918, following a five-hour bombardment and led by thousands of highly trained storm troops, three and a half German armies broke through the British Fifth Army lines south of Arras. They made gains that had not been seen since 1914, but the exhausted soldiers couldn't keep going, and supplies and supporting artillery couldn't get to them over the devastated battlefields. In two weeks, the attack ground to a halt in front of Amiens, with each side suffering 250,000 casualties.

On April 9, the Germans tried again around Ypres, and then three more times against the French between May 27 and July 15. Each time, there was an initial breakthrough, but the rapidly tiring and poorly supplied soldiers were unable to maintain the assault long enough to force a decision. As the fifth attack stalled, the German High Command called off the offensive on August 7.

By now, the Americans were in France in large numbers and the British and French had had a chance to build up their own resources. On August 8, it would be their turn.

65

The Calm Before the Storm

After Christmas, Russell was given a new job painting crosses with the names of the thirty-three battalion dead from Ypres. He began his task on his twentieth birthday, January 1, 1918. The work took Russell into February because he also drew sketches of the crosses to send to the soldiers' relatives. But even while he was commemorating those killed in October and November, the need for more crosses went on.

THURSDAY, JANUARY 3, 1918
"A" Company got hit bad last night. Twelve casualties—two killed, four not expected to live. Cleverdon, Brennan [were killed]; Salvage, Anderson, Smillie, Snelling, Wagg, Felpot [were] wounded. Ten casualties on the way up to save two.

At the beginning of March, Russell was given the job of batman to Company Major Lytle. Essentially, he was to be the officer's servant—a job Russell didn't like at all. By the fourth day, he was in open rebellion and prepared to go into the front-line trenches instead.

SUNDAY, MARCH 10, 1918
I'm fed up with batting—already it's on my nerves. I was supposed to be on at the mess but didn't show up. Quite willing to go out in the ranks if they don't like it.

The next day he again failed to show up at the mess, but his rebellion was a losing battle. On March 12 he recorded, "Had to give in today." But Russell's petty troubles with army life were about to become insignificant. He was fortunate not to have been a part of the British Fifth Army, but even where he was, there were signs that something was about to happen.

FRIDAY, MARCH 15, 1918

Fine day and air very active.

SUNDAY, MARCH 17, 1918

Frizs had fourteen [observation] balloons up with our guns popping at them, trying hard to bring them down. A few prisoners were taken last night. I saw five going down the road.

WEDNESDAY, MARCH 20, 1918

Rainy first day at Berthonval Farm . . . We ended the night with a good old sing-song. Guns a little more active toward night.

The Storm

The morning after Russell's "good old sing-song," a huge German attack began to the south. The shelling and bombing were everywhere, and it was a time of great uncertainty, with men waking up in the middle of the night expecting attacks and moving at a moment's notice.

THURSDAY, MARCH 21, 1918
Frizs started his offensive during last night, shelling all back areas and fighting on a fifty-mile [eighty-kilometre] front with thirty divisions. During the day he captured four villages and bent the line in different parts. His casualties are estimated at seventy-five thousand men. Guns still very active.

TUESDAY, MARCH 26, 1918
The guns back of us very active. Frizs airplane [flew] very low near us in afternoon, taking observations. Machine-gun fire drove him back. His plane fell just at the aid trench. Both men [were] taken prisoner, unscratched . . . Burket, S.B. Brown, Sig[naller] F. Lee, and Sloan wounded today. Sloan died.

Throughout this period, Russell and his mates moved around a lot, and they were sometimes left without supplies.

THURSDAY, MARCH 28, 1918
Got permission to go up to [the] winter trench for blankets. Thélus being shelled too bad, couldn't get through. Dead lying on road, so had to come back.

The next day, Russell tried again, but with no better luck. Because of a heavy barrage, he couldn't get through, and this time he saw "three men lying dead, two being carried off." Finally, on the last day of the month, he managed to get the blankets he was after.

Applauding
the Enemy

The German air force made a priority
of bringing down British observation
balloons so the Allies wouldn't be
able to see what their opponents were
preparing to do next. Observation
balloons were tempting targets for
enemy pilots, but bringing one down
was no easy task. The balloons were
protected by Allied fighter planes and
by anti-aircraft fire from the ground,
and they often could not be brought
down with conventional bullets.

TUESDAY, APRIL 2, 1918

Things still going hard, fine day for observation. Frizs shot one of our balloons down at 1 p.m. At about 6 p.m., one of his planes came over low and got one of our balloons, then went for the second and got it, then for the third. A barrage [of anti-aircraft fire] was put up in front of it, but he got through and got the [third] balloon, then the fourth. They pulled it [the fourth balloon] down and then put it back up, and he came back and got it. Got away.

The official battalion diary called the destruction of four balloons by one pilot "a most daring coup . . . a record feat so far as anyone knows," and in his 1977 diary, Russell recorded that "the troops cheered the German, and everyone wished him a safe return." The soldiers that day were applauding the pilot's skill and bravery— qualities that were respected on both sides of no man's land. And it helped that, as the battalion diary also noted, "so far as could be seen, all the observers made successful descents from the balloons in their parachutes."

Quieter on the British Front

As the German attacks on the British section of the front ran out of steam in May, things quietened down a bit in Russell's area. The shelling and occasional casualties continued, but there was still time for baseball, games of chance, and concerts. There was even a moment to go for a swim, although that too could be dangerous.

THURSDAY, MAY 23, 1918
Came in at 4 a.m. as it was raining. Musketry in morning, then paraded down by mill and had a swim. Women were passing, so of course the boys just camouflaged themselves.

After his short-lived spell as a batman, Russell was back at work sketching maps, dugouts, and graves, as well as designing menus for regimental dinners, an activity that fills several pages of his diary. He even sketched his billet, but it too turned out to be a dangerous place when a piece of shell whizzed by, making his "fourth real close shave so far."
   A few days later, as part of a reorganization, the 123rd Battalion was broken up and Russell found himself in the 7th Battalion, Canadian Engineers.

FRIDAY, MAY 24, 1918
King's birthday, no parade. Slept in till 11 a.m. Raining off and on through the day, so we cancelled boxing bouts and concert at night. This is the last day the 123rd Royal Grenadiers hold as a unit. Tomorrow "A" Company and a third of "D" become the 7th Field Engineer Battalion, "B" the 18th, "C" the 9th.

SATURDAY, MAY 25, 1918
Packed up and paraded to HQ, had speech by Colonel [Walter] Kingsmill. He broke down and couldn't finish.

The 123rd Battalion had been together for two and a half years and its breakup was, according to the last entry in the battalion diary, "a very heart-rending blow to all members of it."

Omens

As the war dragged on into summer,
Russell and his mates began to notice
that more and more of them were
falling sick.

FRIDAY, JUNE 21, 1918

Manoeuvres today . . . J.M. Sperise came home sick and
went to bed. [He's] got the same complaint [as] 250 RMRs
[members of the Royal Montreal Regiment], are parading
sick with throat trouble.

SUNDAY, JUNE 23, 1918

Divisional sports at Linghem [a small village near where
they're billeted]. Boxing, racing, jumping, midway, etc. . . . Our
baseball team won from the field ambulance 14–27. CMR
[Canadian Mounted Rifles] has a sick parade of 250 in one day.

MONDAY, JUNE 24, 1918

An epidemic of influenza has got the troops and civilians;
it's also in England. Ambulance going to and fro all the time.
A great number of cases in the battalion.

Soldiers were told to gargle their
throats at suppertime to avoid getting
ill. On June 26, the battalion diary noted,
"There is a serious epidemic of a three-day
fever in the Regiment . . . Strikes the
men very suddenly, and after about three
days leaves them just as suddenly. It
appears to be a violent form of influenza."

What Russell was witnessing was the
first wave of an influenza pandemic that
was sweeping the world. The huge numbers
of people from all corners of the globe,
crammed together in camps and trenches,
contributed to the spread of the disease.
What he experienced in June seemed like
a normal epidemic, but the flu would
return at the end of the summer and again
in 1919 to kill somewhere between fifty
and a hundred million people. In Canada,
fifty thousand people died—almost as many
as were killed in the war itself.

Final Preparations

The British front remained quiet through July.
On the eighth, Russell noted that he had been in France
for sixteen months. Around this time, there was a
poignant incident that he didn't record in his
wartime diaries, but it stayed in his memory and he
made mention of it in the book he published privately
in the 1970s. "Walking up the street," he wrote then,
"I picked up a youngster who had just blown his
fingers off with a detonator." A doctor who examined
the boy "found eight more [detonators] in his pocket,
enough to blow three or four of us up."

   Later in the month, Russell and the 7th Battalion
moved closer to Amiens, where preparations were in
full swing for a major Allied offensive.

TUESDAY, JULY 16, 1918
Tait and I got a good soaking last night. It rained hard.
We started in first thing this morning on a dugout for two.

THURSDAY, JULY 18, 1918
Got word today we were moving again tomorrow to forward
billets . . . Was detailed for night party, working in no man's
land on light railway.

Soldiers from all over the British Empire
were being collected for the coming battle.

FRIDAY, AUGUST 2, 1918
Australians [are] looking for fights with the
Canadians, and they're getting their share of it.

SATURDAY, AUGUST 3, 1918
Australians very tough . . . fighting with the
Canadians all the time. Americans not bad sports
at all. Lots of traffic going through the town.

WEDNESDAY, AUGUST 7, 1918
The bunch go over the top in the morning, one
constant string of traffic . . . All roads are to be left
clear. A bunch of tanks went up. Lieutenant
Thompson and a party of "C" Company go over
with two tanks in the morning.

PART FIVE

THE LAST HUNDRED DAYS

AUGUST TO NOVEMBER 1918

THE PATH TO VICTORY

After the Germans had exhausted themselves, it was the Allies' turn to launch an offensive. On August 8—after carefully amassing vast reserves of guns, tanks, munitions, men, and supplies—they attacked outside Amiens, France, the point the Germans had reached in March. The Canadians and Australians broke through and advanced farther in one day than anyone else had in four years of warfare. Russell's diary entry for that day was triumphant: "4 a.m. the boys went over the top . . . During the day made a nine-mile [fifteen-kilometre] advance, taking seventeen thousand prisoners right along the line."

August 8 was the beginning of the Hundred Days Offensive, the final charge that ultimately ended the war. German soldiers began to surrender in massive numbers, and one of their top generals called it "the black day of the German army."

A major factor in the success at Amiens was the use of hundreds of tanks and the sophisticated ranging of the heavy artillery. But by August 13, the British were suffering the same problems that the Germans had faced in their spring offensives: the men were tiring, the tanks were breaking down, and the artillery was moving up too slowly. Unlike the Germans, though, the Allies had the resources to open new offensives elsewhere. There was still a lot of hard fighting and hundreds of thousands of casualties to come, but after Amiens, everyone knew that the final goal was in sight. On November 11, 1918, while the Canadians were fighting in Mons, Belgium, where the British had first gone into action in 1914, the war came to an end.

Open Warfare

Throughout August, Russell recorded seeing prisoners taken by the hundreds and German dead everywhere he looked. Led by the Canadians and the Australians, the Allies had finally broken through the front lines and were fighting in open country. As the Allies burst through the German defences, Russell and his fellow soldiers rushed to keep up with the advance.

FRIDAY, AUGUST 9, 1918
Still going hard, prisoners coming down by the hundreds . . . The whole corps [is] moving up with the advance. Thousands of troops and transports coming in reserve.

SATURDAY, AUGUST 10, 1918
Still going ahead. [The Germans] bombed last night pretty hard, killing Lieutenant Knowles . . . Heavy casualties coming down today and more prisoners.

SUNDAY, AUGUST 11, 1918
A bunch more tanks and armoured cars went up today. The French are mixed right in with us now, all fighting together. Bombed heavy at night, killing 107 DAC [divisional ammunition column] mules.

With the return to open warfare, the cavalry came back into its own for the first time since 1914. Small, fast tanks called Whippets, a newer weapon of war, also proved their use on ground not turned into a swamp by shelling. Russell saw the two-men tanks attacking and understood the important role they had to play in this offensive. But even these armoured vehicles offered their crew only limited protection. "As we watched them going forward," Russell noted, "a direct hit was made on one tank, killing both men."

By late August, Russell was on his way back to Arras, travelling on crowded boxcars or marching all night in the rain.

Moving Forward

The fighting was intense around Arras, where it
took longer to achieve a major breakthrough. The
7th Battalion was working so close to the front
lines that the men were in constant danger.

SUNDAY, AUGUST 25, 1918

Up at midnight, fell in battle order with pick or shove l . . . Moved off at 4 a.m. to Feuchy, on the Scarpe River. [The Germans were] shelling the town bad. Lieutenant Ewart got killed, also Leicester, the stretcher-bearer. Three others wounded.

When he draws the scene after the war, Russell adds more detail. "We were in the middle of [a German] counterattack. Took shelter near a house. While Lieutenant Ewart was directing us to trenches, he was killed, as was Leicester . . . Three others were wounded . . . I lost my rifle while racing to the outskirts. My brother called me to take cover. Was I glad to see him."

Nearing the End

As Russell worked his way east behind the
advancing army, it became more and more obvious
that the war was finally going to end. The
Germans were destroying everything that might
be of use to the Allies, and in every village,
there were wild scenes of celebration as
delighted civilians welcomed their liberators.

MONDAY, OCTOBER 21, 1918

Pulled out again this morning. Walking the railway track passing Somain, a big railway centre. Every joint in the track [is] blown, all switches, etc. . . . Entirely new railway will have to go in. We came right through to Wallers . . . Civilians greeted us with cheers, kisses, and lots of coffee. Every house had flags flying.

Despite the celebrations, it was hard going through the devastated landscape. Bridges had been blown apart, and dead soldiers and animals were everywhere.

TUESDAY, OCTOBER 22, 1918

At Wallers out filling mine craters at all the crossroads, which the Germans have blown. On all high points—churches, slag heaps, etc.—he has put up a white flag, meaning civilians [are in the] town.

WEDNESDAY, OCTOBER 23, 1918

Went a little ways further up into the bush [and] filled up some more craters. Fired fifteen rounds at [a German] plane. Came back and all our blankets, bread, butter, jam, soap, etc., was stolen.

Even though it was clear that the war was all but over, the fighting and shelling went on. In Jemappes, a small Belgian town outside Mons, one house was destroyed by a German shell just hours before the end.

SUNDAY, NOVEMBER 10, 1918

Was sucked in by RSM [regimental sergeant major] to move German demolitions. On my way up street, with two bags dry gun cotton, a shell came over [and] hit in back of house. I went in. Two babies hit—one in head, which I took to doctor, other baby hit in arm. A large number of civilians hit today.

Respect and Resentment

Despite the euphoria that came with the end of the war, liberated civilians also felt a lot of resentment toward the retreating German soldiers.

In Jemappes, four prisoners were rushed through the town, guarded by four mounted cavalry with drawn sabres. The civilians, almost out of hand, threw stones and clubs at the Germans. No doubt they would have killed them had it not been for the mounted soldiers.

In nearby Mons, the fighting went on until the very last minute (a Canadian soldier, George Lawrence Price, was killed two minutes before the war ended), and there were bodies from both sides of the conflict lying in the streets that day.

MONDAY, NOVEMBER 11, 1918
As we walked through Mons, ten Canadian soldiers lay dead. By mid-morning, every one of them was covered with flowers, while hundreds of civilians passed by with tears in their eyes.

The last German dead, on the other hand, got none of the "sympathy and respect shown the Canadian casualties, [but] were kicked, spat on and scorned by the civilians."

All Over at Last

On the morning of November 11, things ended not with a bang but a whimper. An armistice, or ceasefire, had been signed and the fighting stopped at 11 a.m. It didn't seem possible that after so many years of horror, it could all be over. But it was, and the memory of that day stayed vividly with Russell all his life.

MONDAY, NOVEMBER 11, 1918
Repairing a bridge since midnight on the main roadway leading into Mons. Coming on daylight, things seemed very quiet. The guns had stopped firing. People began peeking out of doorways, realizing something was happening. The bridge [being] solid enough for traffic, we dropped our repair equipment, picked up our rifles, and headed for town. What a celebration! Thousands of civilians trying their best to do something for you—food, wine, beer. Arm in arm marching further into Mons. Still wondering, Can it really be true?

93

PART SIX

THE LONG ROAD HOME

NOVEMBER 1918 TO MARCH 1919

WHY CAN'T WE GO HOME NOW?

The war was over, but that didn't mean everyone could simply pack up and go home. Millions of men were still armed and in uniform—some victors and some defeated—and it would take time to turn them back into civilians. Besides, there was work to be done, damage to be repaired, and huge stockpiles of munitions and weapons to be cleared.

Men who had fought for years and watched their comrades be killed beside them found it difficult to understand the delay. Many felt they were being denied a chance to go home. The same army regulations these men had accepted as a necessary part of war now seemed petty and annoying. When this was combined with harsh discipline, poor food, and overcrowded conditions, trouble was inevitable.

In January 1919, thousands of British soldiers mutinied in camps in France and England. In March at Kinmel Park in Wales, anger boiled over among Canadian soldiers, furious that ships supposed to take them home had been reassigned to Americans who had not been in Europe nearly as long. In the attempts to quell the riot, five Canadian soldiers died and twenty-eight were wounded. A further twenty-seven were sentenced to up to ten years in prison.

Russell wasn't involved in any out-and-out mutinies, but he felt significant unhappiness at the slow demobilization process. He and the others had done their job and they simply wanted to go home to their families and attempt to recreate a peacetime life.

Sick and Bitter

After the euphoria of the ceasefire,
Russell and other soldiers like him
started to object to the discipline
of army life. Within days, the
pages of Russell's diary began to
show his frustration.

MONDAY, NOVEMBER 18, 1918
Scrubbed equipment at 11 a.m. Was sent to battalion HQ . . . then 3rd Division HQ . . . and was wanted to carry on with drafting but don't want the job.

TUESDAY, NOVEMBER 19, 1918
Working on stencils for GOC [general officer commanding] of all badges of 3rd Division. Don't like the job or the man. Want to get back with the boys.

The next day, Russell was sent for in the middle of the night but failed to show, and he woke up the following day feeling sick and fearing he had influenza. The officers began to take notice of his insubordination.

FRIDAY, NOVEMBER 22, 1918
Sick again, light duty. General raised hell at me not showing up. Was up [appeared] before the adjutant. Explained things, that he [the general] was no man to work for, and [the] insults that he had handed me, and no encouragement whatsoever.

While Russell was feeling sick and angry, Allied prisoners of war were being released much faster than the regular soldiers were being sent home. At war's end, 185,329 British Empire soldiers, including 3,847 Canadians, were prisoners of the Germans. These men soon joined the millions of other prisoners and refugees struggling to find a way home. "Thousands of prisoners, dressed in all types of uniforms, return from the German lines on the roads leading to Mons," wrote Russell in his 1970s diary. Everywhere there were refugees from the war, making their way as best they could.

Christmas in Belgium

At Christmas, Russell was still in Belgium, although he had enjoyed a two-week leave in Edinburgh, Scotland, earlier in the month. It must have been especially difficult to spend another Christmas so far from home now that the war was officially over, but Russell seemed determined to make the best of it.

DECEMBER 25, 1918
Christmas Day. Had our dinner in town hall [in Wavre, Belgium, southeast of Brussels]. Extra-good meal and enough rum. Dance after. Lots of civilians.

After Christmas, though, it was back to endless marching, heavy work, and lice-filled billets.

MONDAY, DECEMBER 30, 1918
Moved off 8 a.m. on the cobbles again. Felt very sore . . . Passed a few German prisoners and ended up in Denderwindeke, [a small Belgian town of] about a hundred population. Any place is good enough for us. So they think because we're supposed to be on our way home.

On the last night of 1918, the celebrations got a bit out of hand.

TUESDAY, DECEMBER 31, 1918
At night, some of the boys were drunk. Getting on for midnight, a brick was thrown thru the window at the officers. It was not found out who threw it.

The following day, Russell celebrated his twenty-first birthday by marching seventeen miles (twenty-seven kilometres). Like all the men around him, he was eager to get home and feeling "very unsettled."

Dirty Buttons
and Hard Work

All through the army, standards were
dropping as civilian soldiers waited
unhappily to go home. On January 7,
Russell was disciplined for having
dirty buttons on his uniform. The
following day, he recorded his
discontent in his diary.

WEDNESDAY, JANUARY 8, 1919
That lowdown dirty Irish sergeant major has me up today
on [guard duty]. The major gave me [extra duty] for the
following night. Had quite a talk with him and was ordered
out of the room. In three years I have not had a crime against
me, and then get [punished] for a miserable six dirty buttons
on greatcoat.

Russell was now skipping out of work
whenever he could. Having been assigned
to two sections, he worked it so that
each one thought he was with the other.

WEDNESDAY, JANUARY 15, 1919
Being attached to two sections, I'm ducking a lot of work. I'm
in five [section] and attached to six [section]—six goes out
and forgets me. Five warns me for parade, [but] I tell them I'm
attached to six, and so on.

He couldn't avoid all work, however, and
what he did was hard—unloading ammunition,
sorting equipment, and moving salvage from
place to place. Like everyone else, Russell
just wanted to go home now that the war
was won.

Prison Labour

February began with
Russell still working
hard, although there
was time for fun in the
winter weather.

FRIDAY, FEBRUARY 7, 1919
Snowed pretty hard during the night. The
Imperials [British soldiers] gave us a good snow-
balling on our way to the dump. On our way back,
we were ready for them with two boxes of ready-
made snowballs.

The Allies blamed Germany for
starting the war and felt justified
in holding on to some of their
prisoners to use as labour in
clearing up the war damage. This
meant that the POWs often worked
beside the Canadian engineers.

Russell and his mates felt
sympathy for the poorly fed men
and shared their rations with them
when they could. Not everyone felt
the same, however, as Russell noted
when, after the war, he revisited
scenes that he had witnessed in
early 1919.

FEBRUARY 1919

It was rumoured many times how badly our prisoners were treated in some German camps . . .
Next to the divisional salvage area was a camp for German prisoners, under the command of British officers and guards, who treated these men brutally and half-starved them.

Arrived in London 8 a.m. Roamed around having breakfast in the Beaver Hut [a YMCA building where soldiers could relax, socialize, and write letters home] and took the 11:10 a.m. train for camp, arriving [at] Bramshott Camp [southwest of London] 12:45 p.m. Got my kit and grabbed three bed-boards and put in the night with a toothache.

MONDAY, MARCH 3, 1919

A little march this morning, rained near all day. Went to hear lecture on tiger hunting and to see *The Female Hun*, a play in four acts and ten scenes. Not too bad.

On March 16, more than four months after the official end of the war, Russell was issued with an embarkation ticket, dispersal area papers, and one hundred cigarettes. The next day, two years and seven months after he had embarked on the same ship in Halifax, he boarded the *Olympic* again.

MONDAY, MARCH 17, 1919

Reveille 5:30 a.m. First bunch moved off 7:30 a.m. We moved 8:30 a.m., leaving [Bramshott Camp] and arriv[ing] Southampton a little after noon. Boarded the *Olympic*. Five thousand troops [and] a larger number of civilians and nurses pulled out 7 p.m. A larger crowd saw us off [with] great cheering.

The *Olympic* Once More

In mid-February, Russell crossed back over to England and had another leave. He returned to Edinburgh and visited the zoo, went to some shows, and reconnected with a girl he'd met on his last leave. After that, it was south to camp in England, where there was more waiting, enlivened by baseball, theatre shows, and lectures.

The voyage over the Atlantic was long, beset by stormy weather and strong winds, and delayed by fog, but the *Olympic* finally docked in Halifax on March 25. Russell remembered, "What a glorious feeling to put foot on Canada again. It's hard to describe our emotions after three years of war . . . Arrived in Toronto 11 p.m. [on] Friday, March 28 . . . Dick and I were warmly welcomed by our relatives. Discharged at midnight. Free men."

ACKNOWLEDGMENTS

Every historian dreams of discovering an old diary forgotten in an attic or an important document misfiled in an archive. My moment came at Pringle Creek Public School in Whitby, Ontario, on Remembrance Day 2013.

I had just finished a presentation on the First World War when the grade three teacher, Melissa Rabjohn, approached and showed me a diary that her grandfather's uncle, Russell Hughes Rabjohn, had published privately in 1977. The moment I saw the diary, a chill shot down my spine—it was filled with the most extraordinary drawings of a soldier's life during the First World War. So my first thanks must go to Melissa for coming up to me that morning, giving me my historian's dream moment, and beginning the process that led to this book.

Russell Rabjohn's family—his son, Robert; grandson Gord; and granddaughter Jan—were unfailingly helpful in telling me stories about him and sharing his family photographs, his childhood sketches and cartoons, and his completed adult artwork. I hope *A Soldier's Sketchbook* does appropriate service to Russell's memory.

The staff members of the Canadian War Museum in Ottawa—particularly Jane Naisbitt of the Military History Research Centre and Collections Information, and Carol Reid and Susan Ross in the Archives—were patient and helpful, and they contributed greatly to the pleasure and productiveness of my two visits to read Russell's written diaries.

Thanks are also due to Tara Walker at Tundra for seeing the potential in this project; to Liz Kribs for shepherding it along and answering my dumb questions; to Janice Weaver, whose precise yet gentle editorial hand made this book so much more than I could have managed on my own; and to designers Terri Nimmo and Jennifer Griffiths, who have given us such a visual feast.

Last but not least, I must thank my partner, Jenifer, who once again waited with patience and understanding while I went off to the First World War.

FIRST WORLD WAR TIMELINE

1914

JUNE 28   Archduke Franz Ferdinand and his wife, Sophie, are killed by Gavrilo Princip in Sarajevo.

JULY 28   Austria–Hungary declares war on Serbia.

AUG. 3   Germany declares war on France.

AUG. 4   The United Kingdom and Canada declare war on Germany.

AUG. 23   The British see their first major action at the Battle of Mons.

OCT. 19   The First Battle of Ypres begins.

DEC. 24   British, German, and French troops lay down their arms for the Christmas Truce.

1915

MAR. 10   The Battle of Neuve-Chapelle begins.

APR. 22   Canadian soldiers see one of their first major engagements at the Second Battle of Ypres. This was also the first time the Germans used poison gas.

APR. 25   Forces from the Australian and New Zealand Army Corps (ANZAC) land at Gallipoli, in Turkey.

MAY 7   The RMS *Lusitania* is torpedoed and sinks. More than a thousand civilians are killed.

AUG. 4   The Germans capture Warsaw, Poland.

SEPT. 15   The Battle of Loos marks the first time British forces use poison gas.

SEPT. 21   Pilot Stanley Caws becomes Canada's first air war casualty.

1916

FEB. 21   Germany's Verdun offensive begins. This series of battles lasts until December 16.

MAY 31   The Battle of Jutland, the war's only major naval engagement, is fought off the coast of Denmark.

JULY 1   The Battle of the Somme begins. The British suffer fifty-eight thousand casualties that first day. The results of the long battle are inconclusive, like so many of the battles on the Western Front.

NOV. 7   Woodrow Wilson is re-elected president of the United States on a promise to keep America out of the war.

1917

APR. 6	The United States declares war on Germany.
APR. 9	Canadian troops enjoy a major victory with the taking of Vimy Ridge.
APR. 29	French soldiers mutiny after the disastrous Nivelle Offensive claims many casualties.
JULY 31	The Third Battle of Ypres, better known as the Battle of Passchendaele, begins.
NOV. 7	Russian socialists known as Bolsheviks seize control of the government.
DEC. 6	The *Mont Blanc* munitions ship explodes in Halifax Harbour.
DEC. 15	Russia and Germany sign a peace agreement.

1918

MAR. 21	The Germans launch a massive spring offensive to try to win the war.
APR. 21	The Red Baron is shot down.
MAY 28	US troops take the village of Cantigny, France, the first American battle of the war.
AUG. 8	The Canadians counterattack at Amiens. This was the "black day of the German army."
NOV. 10	Canadian forces liberate Mons, Belgium.
NOV. 11	The Armistice is signed, bringing the war to an end.

INDEX

FURTHER READING

There is no shortage of good resources for those who wish to delve deeper into Russell Rabjohn's war. One of the best single-volume histories is *The First World War: The War to End All Wars* by Peter Simkins, Geoffrey Jukes, and Michael Hickey (Osprey Publishing, 2003). *Voices from the Great War* by Peter Vansittart (Penguin, 1983) is an oral history giving perspectives from all sides. It's a long read, but the best book on what a First World War soldier's life was really like is *Tommy* by Richard Holmes (Harper Perennial, 2004). For the Canadian experience in the area where Rabjohn spent much of his war, there's *Vimy* by Pierre Berton (Penguin, 1987). My own brief, highly illustrated overview, *Desperate Glory: The Story of WWI* by John Wilson (Napoleon/Dundurn Publishing, 2008), is a good starting place for younger readers. Internet resources include the Canadian War Museum (www.warmuseum.ca), where Rabjohn's diaries are kept; Historica Canada's Memory Project (www.thememoryproject.com); the multimedia site firstworldwar.com; and the British Imperial War Museum (http://www.iwm.org.uk). Any of these will lead the reader to a host of specialist sites that will more than satisfy even the most enthusiastic amateur historian.

LIVERPOOL
NORTH SEA
ENGLAND
NETHERLANDS
GERMANY
LONDON
FOLKESTONE
SOUTHAMPTON
BRIGHTON
BRUSSELS
YPRES
BOULOGNE
BELGIUM
ENGLISH CHANNEL
ARRAS
AMIENS
LE HAVRE
LUXEMBOURG
PARIS
FRANCE